nine inch nails

Exclusive Distributors:
Book Sales Limited
8/9 Frith Street,
London W1V 5TZ, UK

Music Sales Corporation
257 Park Avenue South,
New York, NY 10010 USA

Music Sales Pty. Limited
120 Rothschild Street,
Rosebery, Sydney,
NSW 2018, Austria

OMNIBUS PRESS
London • New York • Paris • Sydney

Photo Credits:

Jay Blakesberg/Retna Ltd.
pages 2, 3, 14, 20, 21, 25, 24, 33, 45

Adrian Boot/Retna Ltd.
Page 16

Larry Busacca/Retna Ltd.
pages 12, 13, 18-19

Neal Cooper/Retna Ltd.
pages 46, 47

Melanie Edwards/Retna Ltd.
page 1

Gary Gershoff/Retna Ltd.
pages 8, 10, 35

Mick Hutson/Retna Ltd.
pages 4, 5, 27, 31, 38

Bernhard Kuhmstedt/Retna Ltd.
pages 28 + 29

Eddie Malluk/Retna Ltd.
pages 40 + 41

Tony Mottram/Retna Ltd.
Back cover

Claire Pasta/Retna Ltd.
page 11

Richard Patrick/Retna Ltd.
page 23

Neal Preston/Retna Ltd.
pages 5, 20, 22, Cover

Stills: pages/Retna Ltd.
pages 36, 37, 42

David Tonge/Retna Ltd.
page 48

Scott Weiner/Retna Ltd.
page 9

Lili Wilde/Retna Ltd.
pages 7, 32, 56, 44

Color Separations by Color 4 Graphics,
Milwaukee, WI

Printed and bound in the USA
by Vicks Lithograph and Printing Corporation

Death amongst the Flowers

Woodstock of 1969; appeal to the same emotions and spiritual desire for love and community. But things had changed. While the original event had been declared an official disaster, this sequel was exactly that for very different reasons. The America of 1994 could not have been further apart from that of 1969. No food was allowed on the site, and a small pizza cost $12. Entrance was $120. Pepsi sponsored the event. Alcohol was banned, which meant drug dealers had a field day. American dollars had to be changed for Woodstock money, the only currency allowed on site. It was a corporate disaster. The original had happened almost by accident; thousands of people in the right place at the right time with the right vibe. Woodstock '94 was the exact antithesis of everything this stood for, with nineties cutthroat commercialism devouring any remnants of the original spirit in a malicious dash for cash. And at the head of the crowd, on the vast waterlogged

stage, stood a lone mud-caked figure, braced against the rain that cut into his black clad body, hair clinging to his face as he screamed out lyrics of such venom and bitterness and malevolent wrath, railing against everyone and everything, including himself. The band was Nine Inch Nails, and the man was Trent Reznor. In that single figure stood the personification of why Woodstock 2 failed, of how America has changed in the last twenty-five years, and of why NIN has proved to be such a phenomenal attraction. This was supposed to be "three days of peace and love," yet the highlight was NIN's blast of primordial hatred, self-loathing, and despair. Despite attempts to revive the hippie world of the 1960s, the darker side of human life—the cult of the killer and the omnipresence of violence and hatred—soon usurped these finer emotions, with NIN's muddy hymns of death and defilement being the ultimate symbol of this. It was a powerful concoction—by the start of 1995, NIN was one of the biggest bands on the planet,

Phylogeny of Terror

Founded and named by William Grant in 1682, Pennsylvania became one of the original thirteen United States. Although the Keystone state offers much in the way of history, culture, and national heritage, for a young kid growing up in Mercer, a tiny farming town near Pittsburgh, it was a wasteland devoid of excitement or life. From the age of five, Trent Reznor was brought up by his grandparents following the divorce of his parents. Despite having a much younger sister, his childhood was effectively that of an only child, since he was separated from his sibling for the large part of their upbringing. Pennsylvania's tradition of insular devout groups such as the Amish was mirrored to a degree in Reznor's own strict religious background. This was reinforced by the parochial focus of his formative environment—for example, when locals "moved to the city" they invariably set up in Meadville, with a population of only 14,258. Reznor later told *Rolling Stone* magazine that although Mercer was not a bad place to live, it was limiting: "My life experience came from watching movies and reading books and looking at magazines." At school and as a teenager, Reznor was something of a shy loner, a misfit in an area of the country where sporting prowess and rugged good looks were the keys to popularity and peer approval. He mostly hung out on his own, and he hated classes. Instead, the youngster preferred to spend much of his time in front of the piano, partly because he was forced to learn by his grandparents, but also because he enjoyed music. As he became more accomplished, his desire to play the ivories in whatever fashion took his fancy provoked the disapproval of his elders They had their hearts set on his becoming a professional concert pianist, constantly shoving scores of classical pieces under his nose. Ironically, he was even encouraged to drop out of school, but only so he could practice ten hours a day to achieve this lofty ambition. However, this was not what Reznor liked most about the piano. He enjoyed the way his playing enabled him to articulate his feelings. By his early teens he had realized that this could very possibly be his single ticket out of Small-town, USA: "I was around thirteen when I realized I could express how I felt through a musical instrument." In addition, his pubescent development created a rather less philosophical motivation: "I'd just discovered Kiss, and I knew I wasn't going to get laid studying piano with a nun."

Before he could get laid, either by a member of the cloth or otherwise, Reznor had to go to college and so promptly enrolled at Allegheny, where he majored in Computer Engineering. With his interest in music blossoming all the time, Reznor became even more isolated, and was often labeled a "faggot" as he was uninterested in sports and displayed an overt passion for music. Furthermore, his lack of involvement in the puerile, fraternity-focused social circles made him even more of an outsider. It was clear that academic life was never going to be for him, and after a year he decided to make the break and head for Cleveland, Ohio, some 200 miles north, taking with him no memories of friends from his early days but a burning desire to break all the boundaries that life in Mercer had placed on him. Looking back on his childhood and the restrictive nature of his upbringing, Reznor later told *Kerrang* magazine that "growing up was like being in a camp for eighteen years—you hear there's a world out there, but you can't get there because you don't know where it is."

At the same time that Reznor was heading for Cleveland, there was a new development in the world of music—along with the previously extortionately priced synthesizers becoming more affordable, sequencers for home computers were also breaking through, offering new possibilities in the realms of musical expansion. The resultant batch of new bands using this technology created a fresh and exciting sound, with groups like XTC, Devo, Human League, and the hyperpercussive Test Dept, all of whom easily outpaced Bruce Springsteen and American rock for Reznor's attentions. It was not the electro pop music that Reznor gravitated towards however—Human League's *Billboard* No. 1 "Don't You Want Me Baby" in 1982 paled for him when compared to the cold and remote attraction of their earlier experimental and arcane material written by the original line-up. This harder edged electronic music captivated Reznor and, in his own words, "suddenly music started to make sense."

In Cleveland, Reznor shared a run-down flat with his close friend and future NIN cohort, drummer Chris Vrenna. Here the two lived the traditional life of struggling musicians—ploughing through one dehumanizing job after another, from counter sales in a music shop to

cleaning the toilets at a local rehearsal studio (where Reznor later bragged that at least he had probably wiped up a few famous musicians' "pubes"). Needless to say, he was a poor employee, as he instinctively hated taking orders from anyone else. Back in the flat, peanut butter sandwiches were the staple diet, and the unit of currency quickly became whichever old records they could get rid of, while any spare time was taken up playing in a sorry variety of appalling local bands. During this time, Reznor first heard Ministry and Skinny Puppy, whose early material with its full-on thumping bass lines and strangled megaphone voices came to be seen by many as the genesis of what was later labeled 'industrial'. Shortly after, this amalgam of various styles was further complemented when

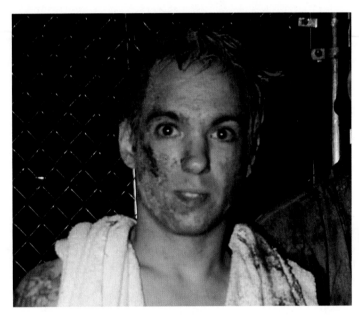

Reznor immersed himself in older music, such as Iggy Pop (circa *The Idiot*), Lou Reed (circa *Transformer*), David Bowie, and the Velvet Underground. The personal and cathartic nature of much of this work reinforced Reznor's growing desire to start writing his own music—up until now he had only really played rock covers. Part of the reason for this was a lack of confidence—he knew of many great pianists throughout musical history who had been phenomenally talented at playing but sadly incapable when it came to original composition. At this early age, Reznor was terrified that this might be the case with him, and he consequently avoided writing anything original for some time. He thought many of his musical ideas were very weird and highly unorthodox, but his lack of confidence was gradually being overtaken by his desire to create. Eventually he called his own bluff and at the age of twenty-three he finally put pen to paper, if for no other reason than to discover if he could do it. It was 1988 and he called himself Nine Inch Nails.

Escape of the Behemoth

Once a musician starts recording original material, the battle has usually only just begun. It is a mark of Trent Reznor's ability and originality that soon after his initial forays into composition he won a record deal with considerable ease. What is even more remarkable is that his debut album was a million seller, despite being released only twelve months after he was stumbling for confidence and unsure if he could write any material of worth. His initial scribblings were made at the rehearsal studios late at night, where his myriad of influences came together to produce the first NIN tracks, and it quickly became clear that Reznor's work would be inherently experimental and predominantly instrumental based. He recorded a basic demo and sent it to a handful of choice record labels, one of whom phoned him. Soon after, a cautious preliminary deal was on the table. Reznor chose to keep quiet about the rapid progress and to let his music do the talking. Even when he did shout, he received little encouragement any-way—he frequently cites Cleveland as the most unhelpful city in America as far as NIN is concerned, despite the band being born there. Once he had an Adrian

Sherwood–produced test pressing of the debut album, he took it to a local club and offered them what was a world exclusive of a band who would later become the hottest thing in America. The DJ snorted his derision, and turned away, saying, "We don't play local bands!"

The debut album, *Pretty Hate Machine,* was released in 1989, and was effectively the sole work of Trent Reznor—the record sleeve itself said "Trent Reznor is NIN." Although he received some production assistance from the likes of Flood, Adrian Sherwood, and Keith LeBlanc, Reznor was clearly the man at the center of the project. The brooding, aggressive opening track, the single "Head Like a Hole" is almost subdued at first, half speed and with slow rhythms, but by the time the second chorus arrives and the guitars crash in with the cruel whipping drums over Reznor's rasping screamed vocals, all hell breaks loose. The rest of the album is an accessible form of techno terrorism, assailing the listener yet clinging on to enough pop form to make it quite palatable. "Terrible Lie," with its staccato beats and mellow tone is still venomous, while "Down In It"

(another single) is funk mixed with utter noise, documenting a sorry fall from grace. "Sanctified" is a bewitching soulful love song, perfectly happy alongside the more somber and even vicious remainder. Perhaps the album's best moment was reserved for the haunting weakness of the near-ballad "Something I Can Never Have," a track that shows Reznor at his most vulnerable, weak, insecure, and sad, delicately treated with a gentle piano drifting over his grizzly vocals. NIN returns to the dance inferno for "That's What I Get," where Reznor reminds us that he is capable of a terrifying concentration of noise. The album closes with the hypnotic "Ringfinger," which cleverly documents the tale of a marriage sealed in blood. The whole record is immersed in a host of salient hooks, slashing guitars, synth noise, technological gimmickry, studio effects, and various samples to complete the collage. There are several weak moments though, such as the sloppy heavy metal of "The Only Time," and "Sin," which is a bad pop song.

Lyrically the record was only competent, not revolutionary, and Reznor could maybe have been a little more dangerous, but overall it was an excellent first effort. Thematically, Reznor displayed his emotional sores, berated former lovers, expressed massive self-doubt, and showed repressed, unrequited love, utter loneliness and insecurity, delivering it all in a lacerated voice. This was the story of the individual against the oppressive forces of the world. The vocal effect was of a howling, uncompromising adolescent fury, riddled with swearing, obscenities, and blaspheming. The debut album scanned the full spectrum of modern dance and super heavy pop, taking angst to new levels and mixing it cleverly with punk and metal and hardcore, making it an adventurous and accessible record. It was an impressive start. It could have doomed Reznor and NIN to cult obscurity status forever, yet it sold a million. Preempted by the difficult single "Down On It," and soon followed by the hard pop of "Head Like a Hole" and the weaker "Sin," the album attracted an unexpectedly large audience, albeit a predominantly dance-based one. Who knows, maybe if "Head Like a Hole" had been released a little later, its rebellion call to youth along with its disco-metal-raw hook may have beaten out Nirvana's "Smells Like Teen Spirit" to become the high note of the decade's ultimate youth battle cry. As it was, the impact was still creditable, and Reznor suddenly found himself the focus of a million eager pairs of ears.

Witness This Barbarity

If NIN's debut recording had been impressive, their first major tour was even more so. The record had hinted at a chaotic world of despair and violence, but nothing could have prepared the unsuspecting world for what was to come once NIN hit the road. For the tour, Trent fleshed out the one-man band with live musicians, chosen more for their attitude than for their virtuosity. In short, the NIN set was terrifying. They frequently took to the stage plastered in white paint or powder, emerging from the shadows as ghosts about to reap manic destruction on the assembled guests. Live, NIN offered Trent Reznor, the shy introverted kid, the chance to exorcise his demons in public, and the fury of his despair and anger was shocking. Often, this volatile concoction lost control and very soon the NIN shows earned a reputation for being a macabre and unpredictable musical time bomb waiting to explode. At one show in San Francisco, the band was struggling against the odds, as one thing after another

went wrong—the monitors were faulty, the guitars kept slipping out of tune, and the mic stands kept falling over. After three songs, Reznor went ballistic. Ripping his guitar from around his neck he smashed it onto the keyboard of James Woolley sending splinters of equipment flying across the stage, before peeling the keys off the synthesizer with his boot heel, like he was picking at a corn cob. After this outburst Reznor simply picked up another guitar and carried on—it was only two songs later when the tour manager ran past and shouted, "It's okay, the medics are here," that Reznor realized anything was wrong. A fragment of guitar had hit keyboard player Woolley, badly lacerated his face and knocked him off his feet, where he had lain on the floor gasping for breath and wheezing blood from spittle covered teeth. Later, at the New Music Seminar in New York, NIN were similarly frightening, and they scared the shit out of the assembled suits and ties by trashing their instruments and then each other during the set. In the autumn of 1991, the band made their debut tour in the U.K., which included a support slot for Guns N' Roses at the famous Wembley Stadium, along with two other stadium dates in Europe. In the U.K., NIN's brand of electroshock treatment won over many new followers to add to the evergrowing legion of fans back at home.

It was wild shows such as these that earned NIN a prestigious slot on the inaugural Lollapalooza tour in 1992. Lollapalooza was the brainchild of Perry Farrell, from Jane's Addiction, a touring package designed to showcase a myriad of musical styles while offering information about a variety of important issues. The idea was to create an environment and forum for debate. At each stadium-sized show there would be stalls organized by major and minor protest groups, such as Greenpeace, gun control lobbyists, and civil liberties groups. Tattooists and fire-eaters added to the general Bohemian atmosphere and the resultant tour package defied the recession and was a phenomenal success—in many senses this was in fact the real Woodstock 2. On this debut bill there were seven bands, and NIN found itself in the middle, following Ice T and preceding Living Color. Despite the array of rich talent on show, it quickly became evident that NIN was in fact the least quantifiable act, and that whereas most of the other bands were

self-explanatory, NIN was the wild card, the loose cannon. As the tour progressed, it became clear that NIN was stealing the limelight from the seminal headliner, Jane's Addiction. The show was a twofold experience (maybe trauma would be a better word). Musically, it was an aural onslaught, an ear piercingly loud primal scream, as the anguish of the recorded work was heightened for the live show. There was little respite from the barrage, with only the two covers of Queen's "Get Down Make Love" and Adam Ant's "Physical" breaking the intense frenzy. The arguments about where NIN belonged in music seemed utterly irrelevant when faced with this howling assault of deranged feedback, monstrous electronic rhythms, and barbaric drumming.

Accompanying this impressive sound was NIN's frightening show itself—a violent, physically draining, and dangerous spectacle. At one show, Reznor stumbled on to the stage screaming madly at the crowd, before spewing water all over the band and crew, unheeded by the threat of thousands of volts coursing through him from the electrical disaster that was waiting to happen. Soon after, he wrapped the mic cord around his neck in an apparently genuine attempt at self-strangulation, which only seemed to galvanize his anger even more. Whipping the cord from around his marked neck, he hurled himself into the guitarist, slamming him violently into the monitors, where his colleague lay crumpled and twitching in agony. Turning to the mic stand, Reznor then hammered that into the drum kit, sending cymbals and skins flying, then ripped the keyboard from its stand, turned once more to the guitarist still on the floor, and hurled it at the defense-less musician. As his victim squirmed to safety, Reznor screamed at a roadie to give him a new instrument, but he had no intention of playing it; instead he then obliter-ated the guitar by pounding it mercilessly into the floor, until it was no more than a tangle of broken wood and frayed wires. Next, Reznor simulated masturbation with a beer bottle and "ejaculated" the alcohol over the discard-ed guitar, before smashing any remaining mic stands across the stage. Then perhaps the strangest thing of all happened, amongst this debris of bodies and gear. A noticeably shaken guitarist walked back on stage and picked up a mic stand, strapped on his guitar and tuned up. At the same time, the keyboard player rescued his instrument from the carnage, clipping it back into place on the stand and rewiring the necessary connections. The crew had been frantically scurrying around stage reorga-

nizing various pieces, and within a matter of minutes the band was launching into another number, as if nothing had happened. Three minutes earlier, Reznor had appeared to be on the verge of permanently injuring half of his band. (NIN smashed loads of gear in this year, but because they were well paid for Lollapalooza they were able to finance this widespread destruction, unlike the Who, who had nearly bankrupt themselves twenty years earlier with their frenzied destructions.) Reznor sees his gigs as a contest between himself and the audience. If at first they seem uninterested, he likes to break through that barrier, no matter what it takes. Some indication of this vicious approach could be gleaned from Reznor's comments in the press, such as when he discussed the legendary onstage ferocity and told NME magazine that "there has to be danger, we have to instill a sense of fear in the audience. Rock and roll deserves that."
While NIN had been emerging as a young band, there was a scene developing around bands like Ministry, Skinny Puppy, Front 242, Revolting Cocks, and NIN, which was labeled for convenience as 'industrial'. None of the bands aspired to or acknowledged that title, but there were certain musical features that gave them a similarity, albeit a loose one. Fearfully hard metallic guitars mixed with throbbing sample-heavy keyboards; maniacal vocals, frequently delivered through a distorted megaphone; and a thunderous and repetitious double bass beat featured on many of these bands' often sinister records. Lyrically the degree of cynicism, bitterness, loathing, and hatred was acute. Shredded black clothing and leather garb adorned the bands and fans, as did multiple body piercing, while a generally apocalyptic tone to their gigs set a morbid and fascinating new movement in motion. Violent moshing was taken to new extremes at many of these gigs, and the stage shows often resembled something straight out of some cult sci-fi B-movie. At the start of the nineties these acts began to shift phenomenal amounts of records and fill concert halls across America. There was clearly some-thing about their approach that was tapping into the music-listening public, and NIN was soon recognized as one of the foremost exponents of this cause. The exagger-ated rage appealed to millions and drew them into their dark hyperreality. It was a music that reflected a time when serial killers had become little more than interesting bar gossip, and where sex and death were intertwined; a feral, sporadic, and nihilistic music straddling the worlds of punk, dance, metal; and grunge. Reznor's production prowess and melodic ear placed NIN at the more commer-

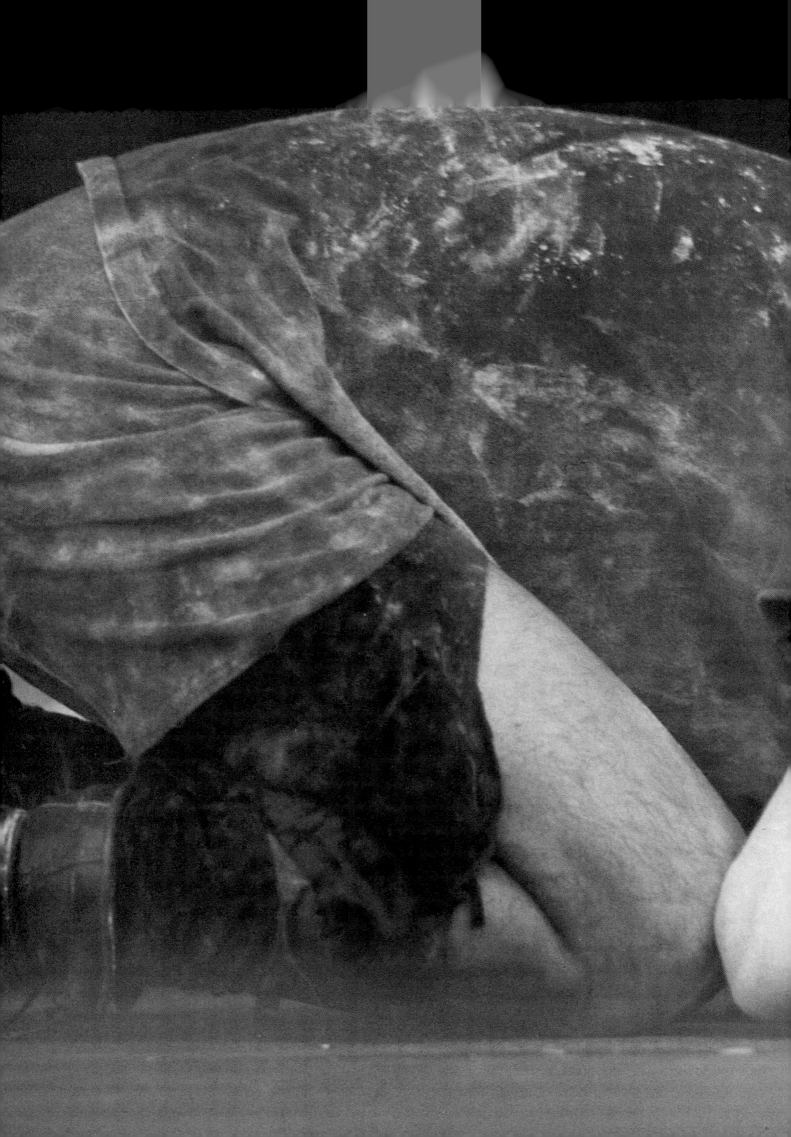

cial end of this movement at this point, although Reznor has always refused to categorize his music so simply. For example, some said *Pretty Hate Machine* had been the first million-selling industrial album. One bad reaction from this period was that some observers said the album was too soft compared to what they had seen on tour, and that the record was a real disappointment. Others saw Reznor as possibly the next metal star. Reznor himself cared for neither of these suggestions and did his best to avoid them at all times. Fortunately, the slot on the inaugural Lollapalooza tour helped NIN capitalize heavily on this growing fan-base and the new interest in this industrial style of music. With the album dates and Lollapalooza completed, NIN had been catapulted to the status of one of America's most hotly tipped alternative bands. The record was still selling strongly, they had moved more merchandise than even Jane's Addiction on the road, and Trent Reznor was being lined up as the new messiah of alternative music. The only problem was that it would be some time before NIN released another album and toured again. In the fickle world of music where the price of bad timing is utter failure, would the world be prepared to wait?

Tyranny, Destruction, & Degradation

The reason for the lengthy delay was not rock-star studio self-indulgence or the rock-and-roll lifestyle taking its toll, but record company politics. With the enormous success of *Pretty Hate Machine,* Reznor's record company TVT had sniffed money and had immediately started to alienate and restrict NIN. As a result, shortly after the album's release, Reznor began to realize that it would perhaps not be in his best interests to remain on that label. The initial problems accelerated when Reznor was asked to guest on a side project with Ministry's Al Jourgensen. When his record company refused because they were concerned about losing their key money spinner in NIN, Reznor was furious. Creative difficulties began to mount after this incident—for example, Reznor wanted to use Adrian Sherwood, the superb producer, for some new work, but TVT refused, saying they had not heard of him and remained unimpressed by his portfolio of production work which included the phenomenal Cabaret Voltaire. These and many other fiascoes forced Reznor to make up his mind—he had had enough and vowed to

break out of the contract whatever it took. Unfortunately, once he looked into exactly what that meant he was horrified. His lawyers advised him that it could take up to two years of litigation and maybe in excess of three million dollars in legal fees, which was way beyond his means, even though NIN had done well with their debut album. He was faced with either recording on a label he hated, or never releasing material again, an option that would send NIN into a tragically early demise. Reznor even considered recording music and giving it away for free. As a middle ground, Reznor refused to record for TVT anymore, but continued with an exhaustive schedule of live dates, including the Lollapalooza tour, an area that the record company had no control over. Unfortunately some critics accused him of milking *Pretty Hate Machine* dry and taking advantage of his fans by not releasing any new material. Eventually he had no choice but to engage in a legal battle with TVT, and it was this protracted war that delayed the second NIN album for so long. Also, this battle meant he had to continue touring as he could not afford to pursue the legal action otherwise. Within the American music industry, the ensuing legal fight is legendary, but Reznor remained unsuccessful in breaking out of the deal.

Sadly, the mental stress that all this entailed took its toll on Reznor, and he was pushed to the verge of a nervous breakdown. The hectic months touring *Pretty Hate Machine,* which the band had undertaken to mask over the difficulties they were enduring with TVT, exhausted them physically and mentally and left them utterly spent. The series of dates would have been daunting enough for most acts, but with the NIN stage show being such a macabre carnival of devastation, the demands were enormous and bound to take their toll. In addition, Reznor's problems were not helped by his separation from a longtime girlfriend around the same period. By now, he had become more insular, much more introverted, and he preferred to avoid socializing if at all possible—he was now a social retard cocooned in his own creative shell. Later on, Reznor even mentioned that he had, at times, come close to suicide.

The musical result of this traumatic time was the unbelievable and disturbing mini-album *Broken,* recorded in secret to avoid interference from the record company.

It was released in the autumn of 1992 and was a six-track record of pure and devastating anger, at times so harsh as to be unlistenable. Despite the rumors that NIN had "gone soft," this record was a shockingly inaccessible release, and yet still went Top 10. The mass of dates in 1990 and 1991 had turned the band harder, and Trent had developed a preoccupation with madly overdriven guitars that gave NIN a maniacally harsh sound. *Broken* was a relentlessly bleak and bitter burst of disgust and hopelessness, an essay in murderous rage, self-loathing and destruction. It was written and recorded between March and August, 1992, in a variety of locations including a deserted hotel-style room near Lake Geneva, a ploy designed to keep it secret from the record company powers that be. Initially, the producer Flood worked on the project, bringing to it the experience that he had earned from working with bands like U2 and Depeche Mode, but Reznor soon took over the reins and completed the record himself. Of the release Reznor said, "*Broken* was a hard recording to make, an ugly record made during an ugly time in my life. I am starting to realize what this is all about, and I don't like it." He also told *Guitar World,* "I wanted to make a real hard-sounding record that was just one big burst of anger. Not necessarily a well-rounded record—just one ultrafast chunk of death." For a man who seemingly had everything, Trent Reznor on *Broken* sounded spiritually destitute, obsessed with railing against the world and himself. With the harsh nature of the content matching the severity of the sound, *Broken* should have been commercial suicide—instead it debuted in the *Billboard* Top 10 and rapidly went platinum. Furthermore, it went on to win a Grammy later in the year, despite one of the lyrics containing the words "fist fuck," no doubt the first time that particular little turn of phrase had been seen as award winning. (Reznor later joked that his epitaph should read, "Reznor. Died. Said 'fist fuck' and won a Grammy.") Critical acclaim was heaped on the record, and Reznor even found himself being asked to produce a Prince track, although he eventually turned this down after meeting the pompous artist and discovering that all the rumors about the purple one's degree of self-love were absolutely true. To the frustration of many of his followers, Reznor announced on the record's release that there would be no touring for *Broken,* which was probably a wise decision bearing in mind the traumas and strains of the previous two years on the road. Reznor was prepared to bare his soul on record, but not to kill himself for ticket sales. The disturbing *Broken* record had a peculiar twin release as well. Entitled *Fixed,* it was a curious remix

album of the tracks on the original. The tracks ran the gamut from conventional to utterly unlistenable, but clawed in yet more critical acclaim. Reznor, it seemed could do no wrong. As if the haunting subject matter of *Broken* was not shocking enough, Trent reinforced his obsession with the macabre by recording video footage for the track that was destined to never see the light of day in any commercial outlet. Visually, the promo for "Happiness in Slavery" was as near to a snuff movie as music videos are ever likely to get. The central theme depicts a naked man (the performance artist Bob

Flanagan) strapped to a torture machine being systematically and graphically disemboweled. He is then further eviscerated alive by a five-fingered metallic claw. The brutal piece climaxes with close-ups of the victim's nipples and testicles being torn off, and all the time there is an uneasy sense of ecstasy about the vile proceedings. Strangely enough, MTV banned the promo.

Despite hearing a defense that the promo was an essay in the resultant ecstasy of submitting to ultimate control, the British censors not only banned it but ordered the record company to take it back to their office immediately and

to never duplicate it nor show it in that country again. Despite his huge success, and the status he had now acquired as one of America's most distinctive writers and performers, Reznor was still being suffocated by the bitter wranglings with his record company. Things looked bleak until shortly after Lollapalooza, when help soon arrived in the form of Jimmy Iovine, who freed him from those shackles. Iovine was a powerful record producer and part-owner of Interscope Records, home of Marky Mark and Gerardo. He desperately wanted to sign NIN but realized that the only way he could get his hands on

Reznor was to buy the record company TVT, which he
duly did. Such was his faith in NIN, that Iovine immediately helped Reznor set up his own record label, called
Nothing Records, and gave him a virtual free reign artisti-
cally. His impressively open attitude to Reznor's work is
perfectly summed up by Iovine's statement, "All I can do
with a guy like Trent is to believe in him and let him go."
The first record released on Reznor's new label reflected
his own idiosyncratic impulse for unorthodox work—a
Reznor-produced album by the Florida group Marilyn
Manson including a song about child molestation that
could be seen as not entirely disapproving. Soon after,
Reznor signed the British seminal electro postmodern
punks Pop Will Eat Itself (it has been rumored that their
brilliant debut album, *Box Frenzy,* and their subsequent
litany of uniquely extraordinary work was a major influ-
ence on Reznor forming NIN in the first instance). He also
signed Coil (led by Peter Christopherson—formerly of
Throbbing Gristle, the band that coined the term and
concept 'industrial') and the postindustrial synth band
Prick. Despite the traumas of recent years, Reznor was
now his own master, and his band's position in American
music's higher echelons was very strong. In addition,
anticipation still remained feverish for the next record,
so things were finally looking up.

Beelzebub and the Pigs

Having received such disapproval over his choice of video for *Broken,* it should not be so surprising that Reznor's next choice of recording would be even more controversial. For the intense sessions for his second full album, entitled *The Downward Spiral,* Trent Reznor hired the house at 10050 Celio Drive, Los Angeles. It was on this spot, twenty-five years earlier (9 August 1969), that Charles Manson's demented disciples had brutally slaughtered the pregnant Sharon Tate, actress and wife of Roman Polanski, along with four others in the absurd and twisted hope that it would incite a race war if the public (as Manson intended) blamed black-power activists the Black Panthers. The killing was as brutal as anything a frequently vicious American society had ever seen before, with the words "Pigs" (as homage to George Harrison's misanthropic lyric to the Beatles' "Piggy") and "Helter Skelter" being daubed on the walls of the killing room in the victims' blood. This tied in with Manson's perverted obsession that the Beatles' legendary *White Album* had in fact contained coded messages to incite race war, or as he termed it, "Helter Skelter." The unparalleled savagery of the murders repulsed America, a nation not easily shocked, and Manson's butchery became a pivotal point of the 1960s. Since then, the murders (and Manson's apparent failed attempts at musical success along with manifold readings of the situation both for and against the dreadful crimes) have been used by various vain and ignorant celebrities to draw attention to their own frail egos. The media themselves have turned Manson into an icon of sorts, the embodiment of evil, the ultimate taboo icon. Thus, when Trent Reznor hired the house for recording his second album, he was immediately denounced for his insensitivity and accused of juvenile shock tactics. Yet, he knew nothing of the house's history until he had paid for it, and he had chosen the site simply because it was beautifully placed overlooking the city, surrounded by lush greenery, and only five minutes away from the infamous Whiskey night club and the Sunset Strip. Once settled into the notorious house, Reznor underwent a very protracted and painful experience writing the album. He locked himself away for weeks on end, never emerging from the studio and isolating himself almost completely from the outside world. His social avoidance increased and was exacerbated by his growing dislike for the sprawling city of Angels below him, and he thus spent at least fourteen hours a day locked away. This isolation gave him the necessary clarity of thought he required to complete the album adequately, but it meant that his ability to relate to others rusted up and retarded. (Moreover, once the album was released and became a success, he would find this intensely personal statement being shared with millions of people and his communication skills so shriveled that he would not really be able to cope with it.) Although his financial security allowed him the luxury of taking his time, Reznor found himself almost completely creatively blocked at first and was unable to record anything. He didn't know what he wanted the record to sound like at this stage; all he did know was that he didn't want a full metal album. He was becoming increasingly frustrated until he spoke to his close friend, the music mogul Rick Rubin, who chastised him for attempting to record substandard work and said, "Don't do it until you make music that it's a crime not to let other people hear." This did the trick and Reznor started to write—over the next six months he completed almost two thirds of the album. The vibe inside the house for him was very sad and quiet, but when added to his own claustrophobic and pessimistic outlook, this began to turn the album into a desperate statement. Reznor dug deep for the lyrical and thematic content and the process was not a pretty one, as he later told *Kerrang* magazine, "This record was an unpleasant experience. It was like climbing down a manhole and pulling the cover over my head." One of the central paradoxes of NIN and Reznor himself is the battle between the desire to create and the desire to destroy, and while he finds it easier to destroy he prefers to create. In combining his own personal experiences and destructive blacker emotions with his creative imaginative projection Reznor came up with an album that was a unique and unnerving document.

By 1994, Trent Reznor and NIN were well known for their nihilistic and angry focus. With the second album, *The Downward Spiral,* however, nobody could have expected just how hopeless Reznor must have felt to articulate such a degree of self-loathing. The record was certainly not short of famous collaborators—it was produced by Reznor and Flood, with guest appearances by Adrian Belew (a guitar guru who has played with Paul Simon and Bowie)

and Steve Perkins (drummer for Jane's Addiction and Porno for Pyros) and was completed by mixer extraordinaire Alan Moulder. Even with all these names around him, Reznor maintained his staunch stance in favor of technology in music, and later said of the sessions, "While trying to avoid the cyberpunk clichés, I like the coldness of electronics. Even if I had the greatest players in the world around me, I'd use a drum machine." One of the key musical influences on the final record was David Bowie's *Low* album (as well as all Bowie's work from *Hunky Dory* through to *Scary Monsters*), which Reznor related to on a songwriting level and which inspired his work from a structural angle. The record shaped up as a loosely based concept album, centered around the theme of a man who is shedding everything around him and has given up on his entire world, his career, his religion, his self-worth, everything—someone who systematically and clinically examines everything then discards it. It became a full-length trip into the depths of human despair, with the antihero eventually self-destructing. From railing against the world, Reznor had now produced a more mature record which fully realized the shift to railing against himself. The album also looks at the various vices that can be used to dull the pain into nothingness—and the violence, paranoia, and misery that this can produce. In many senses these were not new issues to be discussed, but the degree of desperation and hopelessness

that pervaded every track gave the album a unique power. It was a dark descent through self-destruction, through sex, violence, drugs, suicide, and despair, and was difficult but utterly compelling listening.

Musically, *The Downward Spiral* was a break from the past for NIN, with much more attention being paid to the textures, the moods and the subtleties of the piece than had been evident on the earlier breakneck work on *Pretty Hate Machine*. Reznor didn't want to tread on the same ground and slip into danceable synth pop. He had also realized that a whisper can be far more terrifying than a scream, and the resultant dynamics and multidimensions on the record gave it a pedigree that is rarely seen—this was a deliberate ploy by Reznor to avoid getting caught up in the look-how-hard-we-can-play school of macho thought. There was still the ugly humorless noise, such as on the first single from the album, "The March of the Pigs," with its superfast speed and unbelievably malevolent flavor, but this time there were piano breaks in there too. The album has several darker nihilistic moments of quietude—there was the beautiful "A Warm Place" and the childlike repetition of "Piggy" as well. Also, the symphonic splendor of "Something I Can Never Have" showed his grasp of scale and momentum. Not that this meant the album lacked venom. There was still a barrage of industrial techno and furious rock guitar dynamics,

although less so than on *Broken*. This helped to create an eclectic palate when mixed with the vintage synths and raw twisted samples. The album was ingeniously crafted with screaming women, decaying insects, and odd percussive phrases played on the same Mellotron sampler that John Lennon used for "Strawberry Fields Forever." As the album progressed, the sound became more twisted, disturbed, and furious. The sonics and structures of the songs became more incoherent and fractured, reflecting the despairing man's slipping grasp on reality and hope. Overall, this was a much darker sound than the debut album, but completed without resorting to its predecessor's outright noise terrorism. One observer stated on hearing the sonic inventiveness of this record that this was "one of the most violent edged electronic grooves ever to be documented in music."

This hedonistic musical canvas was used to present Reznor's most destitute lyrics yet, but also his best. He was at pains to point out when promoting the album that the lyrics were the most important element of the record, as with all NIN releases. At times he was self-obsessed, as with "I Do Not Want This," but elsewhere

his self-loathing was excessively vicious, as on "Mr. Self Destruct." "Big Man with a Gun" was a suicide gun track that was intended as a parody of the phallo/pistol-centric rap scene and a statement of Reznor's belief that the right to bear arms is an outdated concept (this was inevitably misinterpreted by some). On "Piggy" he crawls inside a serial killer's psyche, the title track explores a suicide fantasy, and with the last track, "Hurt," Reznor hits new heights of intriguing lyrical intensity to finish the record. He admitted that this song was one of the most demanding and difficult he had ever written—its degree of melancholy, sadness, and loss is enormous. As a kid, Reznor himself was frequently very sad and felt alone in that sadness—if people could relate to this piece of work then he would be offering them some comfort in their sadness, a comfort he was denied himself as a child. By the end of the record, everything has been discarded, and the things he looked to for hope have utterly failed him. This was a new breed of dementia. Even Reznor himself knew this was a difficult piece when he said, "As far as *Spiral* goes, all I know is that I made a small-scale, personal, potentially ugly record that reflected how I felt."

Had Trent Reznor been under the thumb of a major record label, his boss would probably have shivered at the thought of a concept album dealing with such harsh subject matter, especially at a time when such things could not have been more undesirable: In the new world of CDs, where the disapproving listener can flick through tracks in a microsecond, Trent Reznor was asking a lot of his followers. Waxing lyrical about self-loathing and paranoia was hardly fashionable and Reznor can rightly claim a degree of pioneering nerve about this in the USA. Furthermore, NIN had shown an ability in the past to produce records that skeptics suggested would finish their careers and yet had in fact escalated them still further. This was to be very much the case with the superb *Downward Spiral*. It was already one of the most eagerly awaited albums of the year when it was eventually released in March of 1994, and it debuted in the *Billboard* album charts at No. 2, going on to take its diseased place in millions of homes across America. The critical acclaim came flooding in, and Reznor was rightly plastered across the front pages of all the world's top music magazines, including *Rolling Stone*. Critics could not say enough about the man's talent and vision, and NIN suddenly found themselves as arguably the most influential alternative band in the world, ironically with a record that was as far from the mainstream as anything they had ever produced. Both of the singles from the album ("March of the Pigs" and "Closer") sold heavily and gave the band more *Billboard* hits. The videos found themselves in heavy rotation on MTV (albeit edited— "Closer" was promo-ed with a grainy meditation on the fetish photography of Joel-Peter Witkin) and the record flew off the shelves. A massive stadium show with Soundgarden became one of the hottest tickets of the year, and the show itself easily took its rightful place as one of the year's best concerts. At one of the album dates in Salt Lake City, Reznor was approached by one man who begged him to meet his friend, which he duly agreed to do, partly because the man had seemed so desperate. His pal was introduced and Reznor noticed he was wearing a hospital wrist-band. He later found out that the man had escaped from a hospital—he only had a

week to live and wanted to meet Reznor before he died. Rumors circulated that he was also receiving mail written in his fans' own blood. His name appeared all over the Internet, with both good and bad things being said, but nevertheless his profile was extremely high. He was asked to, and duly did, appear on a Tori Amos single "Past the Mission" in May, with the vocals again being recorded in the Manson house. One bad reaction for him, albeit a sign he was breaking through to a massive and much wider audience, was an experience he had with the intensely personal track "Hurt." One night he was taken to a seedy strip club at 1:30 A.M. and was horrified to find the DJ playing "Hurt" while the girls disrobed in front of leering, beer swilling men. To add insult to injury, some DJs even wrote to magazines saying how *Spiral* was one of their Top 20 "strip albums" and that the girls were always asking for it as an accompaniment to their act—Reznor was gutted. On a lighter note, Reznor was voted as one of *Playgirl*'s Top 10 Sexiest Men of the year! The extent of the band's success was underlined when the tour dates were announced—having last took to the road for Lollapalooza back in 1992, and in the meantime having risen to the higher echelons of world music, tickets for the dates were like gold-dust. Three massive shows in Los Angeles sold out in twenty minutes and even in the normally reserved hometown of Cleveland, they were all sold out in five minutes. In Chicago, the 60,000 tickets went in just 220 seconds.

There was some criticism of the record, and this took a fourfold nature. Firstly, there was anger at Reznor's choice of studio, as mentioned above. Reznor himself gave little credence to this gripe, claiming he knew nothing of its history and indeed made fun of the whole affair by naming the studio itself "Le Pig." Moreover, the claims that the album had a "pig" theme running through it, and that it was littered with Mansonesque terminology, were belittled by his explanations that "March of the Pigs" was about people he disliked in general, including himself. Reznor also pointed out that "Piggy" was in fact written some months before he moved into 10050 Celio Drive. He quickly tired of this line of questioning and rightly gave it short shrift. The second complaint was that some of his work was misogynist in tone. Reznor defended himself by saying that as a man his bitterness and anger would inevitably sometimes spill over against women, as many traumatic experiences in his life had been with female partners. The third point was that the album offered

absolutely no hope for the listener, and that it was too negative. Cobain, Vedder, and Coughlan all write of despair, but there is an element of hope and redemption in their work. Reznor appeared to offer no light at the end of his tunnel, and he merely snuffed out any optimism in existence at all. Reznor denied it was totally hopeless in vision, and added that even if it was, then it is subjective whether this is good or bad. He pointed out that in discarding all the trappings in his life, the central character of *Spiral* had in fact found some relief and optimism by leaving unnecessary baggage behind him. On this point, he needn't have justified himself—if an artist's personal agenda is full of pessimism and despair then that is what he should write about. Besides, the positive response to the album had been so colossal that these criticisms were swept aside in the general clamor to hail Trent Reznor as the new messiah of alternative music.

At this point, a fourth and more serious debate began to spring up around whether or not Reznor and NIN were for real; that is, was the stage violence and anger just dramatics, was he a fake, another mad-eyed pariah created to revitalize a flailing rock scene that was in need of a new wild antihero? Critics said that it was all too calculated, too choreographed, that his angst was all theater and fake, and that his persona of pain and persecution was nothing more than a calculated sales pitch. They claimed that Reznor's self-mutilation and self-hatred were quite deliberately designed to appeal to a mass audience and that he was not genuinely dangerous. In the words of one critic, "It would never be likely to spill out into a riot on the streets." For these people, Reznor was no more than a clever charlatan, superficial and manipulative, but not truly subversive. Others said he was merely taking the truly avant-garde work of Al Jourgenson and groups like Foetus, Einsturzende Neubaten, and SPK and making them more palatable to the masses, using the paraphernalia of human degradation as fashion items. Some absurdly pretentious critics even went as far as to say he was too macho and hard for these politically correct times, but this was a pathetic argument worthy of no attention. True enough, there may be an issue here, but to be honest, does it really matter if it is all theater? And if it does, how will he ever prove his sincerity, and why should he attempt to? It is a ridiculous argument in many senses, in that the only way he will convince some doubters that he is genuine is by an act of ludicrous futility. If he lay in a pool of his own

blood, the life draining out of his frail body as he slips into a self-inflicted death, there will at least be a few petty-minded journalists running around their office saying, "Oh, O.K., so he was for real after all, nice one Trent." NIN on record and live provides a theater of hate where death and sex are best of friends, where the atmosphere is disturbing and the themes are dark with private and public exorcisms of disgust and despair. Maybe Reznor is more purged than the listener, but so what? Maybe he is just an actor; but if he is, he has succeeded in scaring the pants off the straight world by portraying one of the most dangerous and sick bastards alive in pop. He finds genuine catharsis in his performance, and that is why he is only really alive when performing—his personal purges are for real, as he says himself, "I mean it, but I don't know how I can prove I mean it. I can sleep at night because I know it was honestly how I felt at the time, and I needed to vent that somehow." Yet, at the same time he acknowledges the degree of performance involved: "Essentially NIN is theater. What we do is closer to Alice Cooper than Pearl Jam."

The mammoth world tour for the album gave Reznor a new opportunity to wreak his industrial horror of self-loathing and self-hatred on his audience, most of the set being ripped straight from the womb of Spiral. The response around the world was similarly fanatical, with the British dates in May having to be extended through sheer demand—impressive for a territory that has traditionally been derisive of any form of dance or technological music. In America, two unannounced warmup shows in Hollywood and San Francisco were the worst kept secrets of the year. On the road with him this time, the intrepid musicians were Robin Finck (guitar), Danny Lohner (a multi-instrumentalist Reznor used to fill in any potential gaps in the soundscape, formerly of Texan heavyweights Skrew), James Woolley (keyboards) and Chris Vrenna (drums). There was still the violence against the band, with James Woolley being hospitalized in San Francisco with a broken hand, having had it smashed by a keyboard which Reznor had hurled at him—Woolley had played the rest of the two hour gig regardless. At another show, Reznor had an ex-record-company boss ejected from the premises, screaming wildly at him as he left. On stage this time, the huge global success of the band meant the show could afford to be a little more adventurous, and consequently there was a massive rubber backdrop towering over the stage, with banks of lights and computers swamped in dry

ice crowding the stage. The set invariably started with the mesmeric "Terrible Lie," a slower number that let the NIN experience seep into the crowd rather than smashing them over the head as most would have expected. After that, the onslaught began, with "Sin" and the flesh-peeling "March of the Pigs" taking on a primordial life of their own, replete with blinding back lights and full-on sound. Robin Finck's chainsaw fuzzbox guitars sliced through the mayhem as he snarled at the audience like a wild-haired banshee, proving that NIN can be a dangerously aggressive dance band if they need to. This time around, like the album, there was a more subtle mix of dynamics, with the momentum changing gear constantly. As the extremity escalated, the aural violence was tempered by the quieter "Something I Can Never Have," which was mixed well with the harder "Wish," a contrast that could have easily backfired, but never did The atmosphere changed from oppressive to uplifting without lingering at either extreme for too long. Reznor vocally lurched from shrieks of anguish to exquisite quieter phrases. Some tracks were reworked for the live arena, such as "Reptile," which was more of a riff-o-rama than the much mellower album version. The covers were interesting choices too, with Joy Division's "Dead Souls" being paired with "Suck," which was originally a Pigface track. The criticisms of automatons playing along to click tracks were immediately dismissed, as NIN live is as organic and unpredictable as any show on earth. Reznor himself prowled his own universe around the stage, appearing almost physically small at times, caught in the curious parody of not knowing what is going on in the chaos around him, yet knowing all the time that he is the ultimate controller. He is a thin awkward figure, with his gaunt face and deathly white complexion, against his leather shorts, hair shirt, and oily black hair, but this was the central visual focus of the whole show and you could not take your eyes off him.

The latest NIN show has an outrageously dramatic grandeur, making it a gripping spectacle of hardcore total noise, and one which holds a morbid fascination for the audience. It is almost as if they are rubbernecking some bizarre and gruesome torture, with Reznor as both the victim and the torturer. He stands there apocalyptically silhouetted against the rest of the band, screaming the chorus to "Closer" ("I want to fuck you like an animal"). Hate, fear, terror, sadness, melancholy, despair, violence, blood, and anger mix together in the music, the lighting, the lyrics, and the performance to make this NIN tour one of the greats.

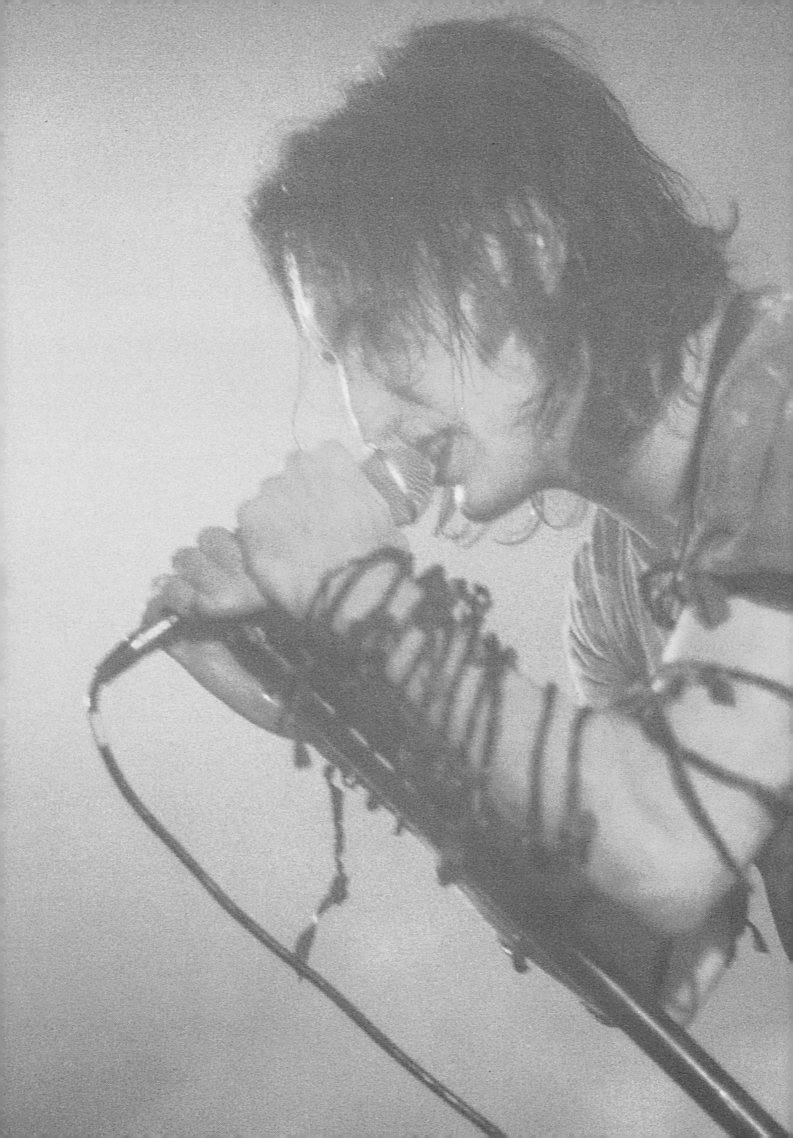

Profanity of the Truth (hurts)

After this monumental success, it would be natural to expect that Trent Reznor would be happy to keep a low profile for a while. Instead, he penned and orchestrated what has been called by some the greatest film soundtrack ever. This is the musical accompaniment to one of the most controversial films of recent years, possibly ever: Oliver Stone's ultraviolent crime fable *Natural Born Killers*, starring Woody Harrelson and Juliette Lewis. Traditionally, movie soundtracks have been inconsistent and often dangerous projects to be involved with. The heritage of hard metal music in violent films goes way back, but with Guns N' Roses "You Could Be Mine" blasting out of a teenage John Connor's stereo in *Terminator 2* a breakthrough was made. With *The Crow, Pulp Fiction*, and *Reservoir Dogs* all producing commendable albums, the form was no longer as questionable as it once had been. Indeed, NIN had been featured on *The Crow* soundtrack, where their cover of Joy Division's "Dead Souls" had played while the camera panned over a Mad Max–style cityscape. This excellent soundtrack also featured contributions from Pantera, Helmet, Rage against the Machine, Jesus and Mary Chain, and the Violent Femmes.

The movie *Natural Born Killers* mocks the American media machine by following the tracks of two serial killers, Mickey and Mallory, whose on screen violence and utter moral degradation was the subject of extreme censors' attention and public concern. Copycat murders occurred (one fourteen-year-old boy decapitated his thirteen-year-old girl pal because he said he "wanted to be like Natural Born Killers"; similar killings have occurred in Paris and New Mexico), and there was a wealth of opposition to the film's release. In Britain, the film was banned for months before the conservative censors finally allowed its release in edited form—even so, the 150 cuts only removed a paltry and unneeded one minute from the running time. It is an ultramodern movie, violent, disturbing, and funny; a vicious satire of the American media and prison system, with its own brand of hypermodern ultraviolence desensitizing the viewer. Trent Reznor came to be involved after Oliver Stone himself phoned him up and asked if he would see the film, so as to agree to the use of some NIN material on the soundtrack. Reznor went to a private showing with a friend in the middle of the afternoon in Los Angeles, and was so amazed at what he saw that he immediately agreed to be involved. At that stage, the soundtrack was under someone else's control and there was a decidedly traditionalist feel to it; Stone asked Reznor if he would be inter-

ested in masterminding the album (and releasing it through Nothing Records) and the NIN man happily agreed. Despite being skeptical of soundtracks in general, Reznor's ideas would isolate what he was to do from any other effort that went before it. Straightaway he set out his goals for the project he wanted the soundtrack to be like the movie, multi-layered and with lots of dialogue, and he also wanted it to be a piece of music in its own right, but one that served to remind the listener of the feel of the movie. In addition, the list of bands to appear on the record was drawn up and was clearly going to be very unusual—the final track listing included music by L7, Patti Smith, Lard, Jello Biafra, Leonard Cohen, Dr. Dre, and of course NIN (the blistering track "Burn" was the one song he was contractually obliged to write specially for the film, and it appeared right at the end, over the final credits). The record was assembled in Europe while NIN was on the European leg of the huge world tour for *Spiral,* a process that was made possible by setting up computers in hotel rooms after gigs and working into the small hours to get the job done (normally on tour Reznor would party long and hard, and only normally calm down when it came to making a record). His efforts were not helped by the lighting computers failing to work as desired early on in the tour, which Reznor then had to spend two days fixing himself. Along with having to watch the film over seventy times, this rushed touring climate added to the hectic and claustrophobic nature of the record, resulting in the cacophony of insane dialogue and diverse sounds on the soundtrack. On returning from the tour, Reznor went to Miami's South Beach Studios, where he had recorded the Grammy winning *Broken* in 1992, to put the final touches to an album which by now had over seventy snippets of music in there. As a distraction to the labors, Reznor screened an S&M video for the assistant studio engineer that left him shaking for days.

The soundtrack itself has a similar effect. It is a complex collage of sounds, music, dialogue, samples, and sound-bites. Cohen's apocalyptic monologues fit seamlessly alongside Dr. Dre's rhythms which themselves are punctuated by screams, endless howls, and gunshots. This mélange is placed next to none other than Bob Dylan. Next comes industrial punk supergroup Lard with Budapest's Philharmonic Orchestra. This is followed by the kitsch pop of Patsy Cline's "Back in Baby's Arms" then proceeding to the hallucinogenic mayhem of Nusrat Fateh Ali Khan's Sufi wail. It is a densely layered aural counterpart to the film's own unique visual appeal, and was a

tremendous opus of arrangements and extraordinary musical collisions. It is simply the greatest soundtrack ever written, and has redefined what the limits of that form are.

Such was the complexity of the record that Reznor had trouble gaining the necessary legal rights, especially since there was so much overdubbing and remixing of original tracks. Interestingly, only L7 proved to be a difficulty, perhaps saying more about their arrogant attitude than any bad review could. There was some criticism in the press, mainly that Reznor was continuing his public fascination with serial killers, an accusation he met head on and denied furiously: "I do wonder what it would be like to kill someone, but I'm not going to do it. But I know why people idolize serial killers." He went on to say, "I'm not personally infatuated with serial killers. I find them mildly interesting at best. I have a curiosity about that, but by no means do I wish to glamorize them." He is, like millions of others in America, part of the small-town disaffected population that Mickey and Mallory came from. He too had railed against the hypocrisy, falsity, and recurrent malice in contemporary American life, only he did so through his music, and through NIN. It is too contrived that he is anything more than that, or that he might go any further. As a rule however, the record received wild applause—the British monthly magazine *Vox* said of the record that it was a "rollercoaster ride of awesome evil jarring jump cuts, intense melodrama and sickening savagery. Queasily unsettling sound effects and peppered with scary snatches of dialogue. Trent Reznor's specially assembled collage of aural carnage only whets the appetite." Despite the continued acclaim this remarkable record earned for Reznor, he was still unsatisfied—soon, after he said, "I'd like to do a real soundtrack. I'm interested in composing, whereas basically this was just editing . . . if we ever manage to stop touring."

Touring is something that NIN seems to do either frenetically or not at all. After all the activity of 1994, they started 1995 by hitting the road for a further two months, this time supported by the Jim Rose Circus Sideshow and Pop Will Eat Itself, probably Britain's greatest band of the last ten years. By now, NIN were confirmed as one of the biggest bands in the world, and Reznor's music had wormed its way into tens of millions of homes worldwide. This entire two-month jaunt was sold out months in advance, and meanwhile the back catalogue of the band was selling continually and heavily. Such was the popularity of NIN at this point.

Insurgence of the Hopeless

Nine Inch Nails is a band that has become more and more brutally uncompromising with each record and with each new success. In many senses, Trent Reznor has completed his career thus far in reverse, beginning with a relatively acceptable pop record and coming to his peak with an album of extreme harshness and a distinct lack of traditional commercial appeal. Even Reznor himself was able to look back on *Spiral* a year later and jokingly say, "I hope I don't get any bleaker than that one. I out-bleaked myself there!" As the band's creative nexus and sole member when not on the road, Trent Reznor is Nine Inch Nails, and it is on his fascinating and complex personality and his wayward and brilliant genius that the band's ultimate future depends. The journey up until this point has been a very circuitous one, and his frail mind has already undergone many strains that would perhaps have been better avoided. But that is the central point about the band—it is the very struggle of life, the battle against the outside world and against himself that makes Reznor's work so compelling. *Pretty Hate Machine* was an admirable debut unleashed on an unsuspecting and largely dance-oriented audience. It earmarked a genuine new talent but only hinted at the venom and spite he can reserve for his environment and himself. With *Broken* he gave us a glimpse into a much darker world, which he controls but which is destitute of hope and inspiration, and musically this record moved NIN forward hugely. With the album *The Downward Spiral* Reznor confirmed the individual ability and talent in full with a work of such dark depravity and desperation, an album that stands alone as one of pop's most devastating moments. Trent Reznor could be just another black-clad antihero in the American cultural tradition, a striking loner railing against middle-class convention and the Establishment as so many have done before him. He could be a calculating business man. He could be just a good actor. Or he could be a genuinely sick punk deviant, despoiling clean minds and subverting the mainstream. More likely, he is the nearest thing yet to a complete video, audio, and literary artist, and stands as far outside the mainstream of this garish popular culture as it is possible to do while selling millions of records. With the success of *Spiral* and the *Natural Born Killers* soundtrack, Reznor has become a cipher for the alternative world, a representative elected by the admiring masses—this could prove to be a compromising and undesirable position for him in the future. He is a pale and vulnerable industrial God for many, even though he denies the term has any relevance to his work. For now, he stands on top of a world that he detests, alone with his own company, which he loathes, and yet his creative direction is as crisp and inspirational as ever. The rude maniacal alter ego on stage is far at odds with the affable and quiet, mild-mannered offstage persona—his vulnerability is as acute as the next man's, he just expresses himself in a passionately vitriolic, aggressive, and extraordinarily creative fashion. He is struggling with everyday life the same way as everyone else is, and the battle scars on his body are testament to the violent way he enters the fight on stage. His is a rare and enigmatic talent, that of an obsessive and harshly self-critical craftsman. Nine Inch Nails was set up to express his discomfort and negative feelings about the world—watching him do this and listening to how he does it has provided one of the most extraordinary spectacles and some of the hardest hitting music of the nineties.

Discography

1989 **Down In It**
CD Tee Vee Toons 2611
Down In It (Skin), Down In It (Shred), Down In It (Singe)

Pretty Hate Machine
CD Tee Vee Toons
TVT2610-2
CS Tee Vee Toons
TVT2610-4
LP Tee Vee Toons
TVT2610-1
Head Like a Hole, Terrible Lie, Down In It, Sanctified, Something I Can Never Have, Kinda I Want To, Sin, That's What I Get, The Only Time, Ringfinger

1990 **Head Like a Hole**
LP Tee Vee Toons 2614
CD Tee Vee Toons 2615
CD Atlantic TVT 26152
Head Like a Hole (Slate), Head Like a Hole (Clay), Terrible Lie (Sympathetic Mix), Head Like a Hole (Copper), You Know Who You Are, Head Like a Hole (Soil), Terrible Lie (Empathetic Mix), Down In It (Shred), Down In It (Singe), Down In It (Demo)

Sin
LP Tee Vee Toons 2617-1
CSS Tee Vee Toons
TVT-2617-4
(contains only last two titles)
CD Tee Vee Toons
TVT-2617-2
Sin (Long), Sin (Dub), Get Down Make Love, Sin (Short)

1992 **Broken**
LP Interscope DMD 1903
CS Interscope 92213-4
CD Interscope 92213-2
Pinion, Wish, Last, Help Me I Am in Hell, Happiness in Slavery, Gave Up, Physical, Suck

Fixed
CD Interscope 96093-2
CS Interscope 96093-4
Gave Up, Wish, Happiness in Slavery, Throw This Away, Fist Fuck, Screaming Slave

1994 **March of the Pigs**
CDS Interscope 95938-2
March of the Pigs; Reptilian; All the Pigs, All Lined Up; A Violet Fluid; Underneath the Skin

The Downward Spiral
CD Interscope 92346
CS Interscope 92346-4
Mr. Self Destruct. Piggy, Heresy, March of the Pigs, Closer, Ruiner, The Becoming, I Do Not Want This, Big Man with a Gun, A Warm Place, Eraser, Reptile, The Downward Spiral, Hurt

Closer to God
CD Interscope 95905-2
Closer to God, Closer (Precursor), Closer (Deviation), Heresy (Blind), Memorabilia, Closer (Internal), March of the Fuckheads, Closer (Further Away), Closer

The Crow (soundtrack)
CD Atlantic 82519-2
CS Atlantic 82519-4
After the Flesh (My Life with the Thrill Kill Kult), The Badge (Pantera), B_ Empty (Stone Temple Pilots), Burn (The Cure), Color Me Once (The Violent Femmes), Darkn_ (Rage against the Machine), **Dead Souls (Nine Inch Nails),** *Ghostrider (Rollins Ban_ Golgotha Tenement Blu_ (Machines of Loving Grace), It Can't Rain Al_ the Time (Jane Siberry), Milktoast (Helmet), Slip_ Slide Melting (For Love Not Lisa), Snakedriver (Jesus and Mary Chain), Time Baby II (Medicine_*

Natural Born Killers (soundtrack)
CD Interscope 92460-2
Waiting for the Miracle (Leonard Cohen), Shitlis_ (L7), Moon over Greene_ County (Dan Zanes), Ro_ n Roll Nigger (Patti Smi_ Sweet Jane (Cowboy Junkies), You Belong to (Bob Dylan), The Tremb_ (Duane Eddy), **Burn (Ni_ Inch Nails),** *Route 666 ("BB Tone" Brian Berda_ Totally Hot (Remmy Ongala & Orchestre Su_ Matimila), Back in Baby_ Arms (Patsy Cline), Tabo_ (Peter Gabriel/ Nusrat Fateh Ali Khan), Sex Is Violent (Jane's Addictio_ Diamanda Gales), Histo_ (Repeats Itself) (A.O.S.),* **Something I Can Never Have (Nine Inch Nails),** *I Will Take You Home (Russel Means), Drums / Go-Go (Hollywood Persuaders), Hungry An_ (Barry Adamson), The D_ the Niggaz Took Over (_ Dre), Born Bad (Juliette Lewis), Fall of the Rebel Angels (Sergio Cervetti), Forkboy (Lard), Batonga Batongaville (Budapest Philharmonic Orchestra Janos Sandor, conductor A Warm Place (Nine Inc_ Nails), Allah, Mohamme_ Char, Yaar (Nusrat Fateh Ali Khan & Party/Diamanda Galas), The Future (Leonard Cohen), What Would U_ Do? (Tha Dogg Pound)*